THE ROMAN RECORD
HOT NEWS FROM THE SWIRLING MISTS OF TIME

ATTENTION CITIZENS

Welcome to your empire-building, slave-driving, barbarian-bashing, lion-feeding, ROMAN RECORD. What we've got here is 1200 years of Roman history in 32 pages of blood-letting entertainment!!!

TROUBLE

We start with the NEWS, and the **founding of Rome** in 753BC by wolf-boy twins Romulus and Remus.

What next? From 510-31BC we report on the **Roman Republic** when we're ruled by consuls and senators, and start to take over the entire Mediterranean.

After that, from 31BC to 500AD, we look at the **Roman Empire** at the height of its powers, when we rule most of the known world, until we're knocked off our perch by a pick-and-mix assortment of barbarians.

It's not just battles and bloodshed. We've got 13 pages of FEATURES – all those daily-life kind of things that make us Romans so intriguing.

CURIOUS

We're a curious bunch. We're so civilized we've got central heating, roads, apartment buildings and fast food eateries. Our temples, aqueducts and amphitheatres are so well built that many of them will still be standing in the 21st century.

We conquered the entire Mediterranean, and most of western Europe. Yet we don't really care what race you are as long as you're a loyal citizen. Some of our Emperors even come from Africa or Spain.

But we've got a darker side too. Our idea of heaven is a packet of salted nuts, a front seat at the amphitheatre and a sunny afternoon of gladiator fights and executions for entertainment. (Find out about these on page 30, gore-fans!) And if you get on the wrong side of us, we'll raze your cities to the ground, sow salt into the earth to stop anything from growing, and kill YOU, **and your pets**, with chilling efficiency.

Happy reading!!!

Catullus the Elder

**Catullus the Elder
Editor,
The Roman Record**

THE ROMAN RECORD

was written by
Paul Dowswell

and designed by
Karen Tomlins

Historical consultant
Charles Freeman

With thanks to Fergus Fleming (Text), Laura Fearn (Design) and Guy Smith (Illustrations).

NEWS

FEATURES

DOUBLE TROUBLE!!
WOLF BOY KILLS TWIN THEN FOUNDS CITY

The twins pictured with their mother. Such adoptions almost always end in tears.

753BC

Here's the good news: Rome has been founded by Romulus. And here's the bad news: he's killed his twin brother Remus in an argument over where the city should be.

The troublesome twosome have been in the papers ever since it was sensationally revealed that they had been brought up by a wolf. Welfare workers are concerned that they may not have a stable enough background to found a major capital. Recent events have only increased their doubts.

SPOT

Romulus spoke to our reporter. "What are you all moaning about? I've given you a world-class city, in a beautiful spot on seven hills by the River Tiber. It's far enough upstream to be safe from pirates, and it's bang on all the major trade routes so it's going to become phenomenally wealthy. What else do you want me to do? Build it in a day?"

SQUEEZE

When pressed about the slaying, he replied: "This town wasn't big enough for the two of us. Anyway, I was fed up being a twin, all those people going 'Are you you, or your brother?' and 'when you were naughty at school did the other one get the blame?' Well this is certainly one murder I won't be able to blame on Remus!"

The twins are well known local celebrities. Sons of Rhea Silvia, a vestal virgin, and Mars, the god of war, they were adopted by the wolf after a wicked uncle threw them in the Tiber.

RARE

Attempts by the *Record* to trace the twins' wolf mother have not been successful. However we did speak to city social service chiefs who issued this statement. "The twins' mother is believed to be living in a forest just south of the city, and does not wish to speak to the press. However, we would like to take this opportunity to point out that animal/human adoption is not encouraged. Experience shows that most adopters eat the children in their care rather than suckle them. Romulus and Remus were an exceptionally rare success."

TARQ'S A GONER

KING THROWN OUT AS CONSULS TAKE CONTROL

509BC

It's ALL CHANGE in today's hurly-burly modern Rome,

Blazing saddles! A couple of consuls lead the way.

as citizens say GOOD RIDDANCE to kings and A BIG HELLO to consuls.

KING SIZE

Ever since wolf-boy Romulus declared himself king, Rome has been run by a bunch of snooty royals. This hasn't gone down well with your man in the street, especially as some of those kings haven't even been Roman – they've been Etruscan!

So who are they? They're the bunch who've ruled most of Italy for the last three centuries, that's who. True, we've learned a lot from them. We've taken up their alphabet, copied their drainage systems and started wearing their funny toga outfits. In fact, thanks to them we've established ourselves as the Numero Uno city in Italy.

BOOT

But now we've had enough. Current king Tarquin the Proud, also an Etruscan, has been such a twerp that top citizens launched a *Boot-out Tarq* campaign and **EXPELLED** him.

Now instead of a king this is what we've got:
•**Two consuls.** The top men in government. They're elected every year for one year only, to lead the senate, command the army, and keep an eye on each other.
•**Senators.** A group of 100 or so people selected from Rome's poshest families. They've got the job for life. Senators meet together in the **senate**. Top government jobs such as judges, tax collectors and financial controllers are all filled by ambitious citizens, but they have to be elected to these posts. All citizens are allowed to vote, and competition is FIERCE! **The Record says: A Roman "nose" best. If we want to be a Republic, that's what we'll be. Consuls and senators will do us very nicely for at least the next 400 years!**

OUFF! BLAT! POW! OUCH!

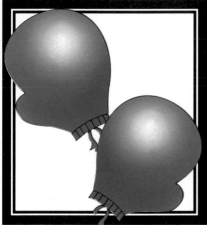

PLEB
REVOLT SPARKS CHANGE AT TOP

PATRICIANS V PLEBEIANS

366BC

Class warfare has erupted in Rome. In the blue corner – *the Patricians*, the heavyweight people who run everything. In the red corner – *the Plebeians*, flyweight ordinary folk. **SECONDS AWAY!**

ROUND ONE
509BC
Ding, ding!

Patricians fill the Senate and govern Rome. It's almost impossible for anyone else to get into politics. THUNK!

ROUND TWO
494BC
Ding, ding!

Plebeians hold violent political demonstrations and strikes. They're protesting against such bottom-of-the-heap ailments as starvation, debts and no land to farm. They also demand more of a say in how Rome is ruled. When this is refused, Plebeians withdraw from the city to set up their own **Popular Assembly**, and elect representatives called **Tribunes** to look after their interests. BOP!

ROUND THREE
450BC
Ding, ding!

Plebeians insist that a full list of laws be written down by the Senate. These are published as the so-called **Twelve Tables**. This stops senators interpreting the law as they please, to suit themselves. WALLOP!

ROUND FOUR
449BC
Ding, ding!

Patricians give the Pleb Assembly the power to stop any law passed by the Senate. SMASH!

ROUND FIVE
367BC
Ding, ding!

Plebs win the right to stand for official government positions, and the first plebeian consul is elected. BLATT!

ROUND SIX
287BC
Ding, ding!

The Popular Assembly is allowed to pass laws, as well as block laws passed by the Senate. OOUFF!

KNOCKOUT!

Political correspondent Servius Sleazus writes: What a match! The Patricians were up against the ropes and they just couldn't bounce back.

The result throws the old system out of the window. The Patricians have learned that it's easier to give the Plebs a say in government than waste energy trying to batter them down. From now on, the best men can rise to the top no matter where they come from.

PAGE THREE COMMENT

ROME
NOT BUILT IN A DAY – IT'S OFFICIAL

264BC

What a scorcher! The past 200 years have been red-hot as we've sizzled our way to success and taken over THE WHOLE OF ITALY.

Mind you, it's not been easy. First we had to show the locals who was who. Then we had to trample all over the Etruscans and their central-Italian allies the Samnites. And what with seeing off a few Celts (*Surely "paying them off to go away before they utterly destroy you?" – History Ed.*) then crushing Greek colonists and some other ragamuffins in southern Italy, we've had our work cut out.

So why are we the best? Two reasons...

•**We're the dirtiest fighters**. Our army is the most disciplined, largest, and the most

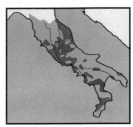

Here we are, spreading like ivy! (We're red, our allies are green.)

unpleasantly ferocious in the world. When we ransack a city, we even cut the DOGS into pieces, never mind the population.

•**We're generous**. After we've conquered anyone, we offer them an alliance. They supply us with soldiers, in exchange for our protection and the fruits of any further conquest. Not a bad deal!

Now that we've defeated our rivals in Italy, you'd think we'd feel like a rest. Not a bit. The *Record* says **LOOK OUT, THE ROMANS ARE COMING!!!**

ROME MAULS

CITY RAVAGED AS TOP-DOG GRUDGE MATCH GRINDS TO GRISLY HALT

146 BC

The Punic* Wars are finally over. At long last Rome has beaten chief Mediterranean rival Carthage. Top general Scipio Aemilianus has made the following announcement: "During hostilities in the Third Punic War, Carthage has been destroyed. This means that WE ARE NOW TOP DOGS AROUND HERE AND ANYONE WHO DISAGREES IS IN BIG TROUBLE.

"To show that we mean business we've burned Carthage to the ground, slaughtered most of the population, and sold the remaining 50,000 still alive into slavery.

"Even as I speak soothsayers are wandering among the ruins, howling and muttering curses to prevent the city rising from the ashes. And just to make sure, we're tilling the

Carthage gets toasted.

rubble into the ground and sowing the furrows with salt. In fact we're doing such a thoroughly horrible job, even I, supreme destroyer of Rome's greatest enemy, feel just a little guilty about it."

END

Scipio's statement ends a 120 year, three-round struggle between Rome and Carthage. To mark the occasion we've gathered together a collection of cuttings from our archives so you can relive those glory, gory days of the FIRST AND SECOND PUNIC WARS once more. Happy reminiscing, readers!

* Punicus is our word for Carthaginian, Latin fans.

Next week: Scipio – "I did it my way" First hand accounts from the front.

FIRST PUNIC WAR 264-241BC

MESSANA MAMERTINES SPARK CLASH WITH CARTHAGE

264BC

The Mamertines – a bunch of Italian bully-boy mercenaries – have seized the Greek settlement of Messana in Sicily. AND THEY'RE NOT GOING TO GIVE IT BACK.

The Greeks have appealed to their pals in Carthage to help them. The Mamertines in turn, have asked Rome to support them. Add it all up and you've got the start of the First Punic War!

THAT'S RICH

So who are the Carthaginians? The *Record*'s foreign correspondent Travellus Chequio explains: "Carthage is this very rich city in North Africa. It's been there for 600 years, has a massive navy, and is at the heart of a thriving empire which goes all along the North African coast, and includes parts of Sicily, Sardinia, Corsica, and the tip of Spain. Stop falling asleep at the back there!!"

COPYCAT CLAIM LEAVES ROMANS UNRUFFLED

256BC

Rome has made a shock breakthrough in the First Punic War with a series of stunning naval victories. After eight years of deadlock where we were better at fighting on land, but the Carthaginians ruled the sea, military bosses in Rome hit on the bright idea of building some ships.

"We didn't have a navy," one sailor told us, "in fact we didn't even know how to build a warship.

Luckily, the Carthaginians stranded one of theirs on a beach, so we found out how it was made, then built 100 identical copies in 60 days, and added a new feature of our own. It's called a *corvus* and it's a big spiked gangway which you drop onto the enemy ship. Then your soldiers can pour aboard and thrash the crew. Works a treat!

"Our navy has remained completely unruffled by sourpuss Carthaginian taunts of "Copycat! Copycat!", and the stage is now set for a knockout blow to Carthage."

Our boys in action.

ROUND-ONE TO ROME AS CARTS LICK WOUNDS

241BC

The curtain's come down on the first Punic War and it's splints and bandages all round.

Our expected massacre of Carthage turned into a series of thousands-feared-dead defeats, in which our brand new navy was wiped out.

REELING

But the Carts took a battering too. We built a new navy which soon sank theirs. And Roman troops have captured Sicily.

Analysts predict a return bout when both sides have stopped reeling.

PUNIC WAR SPECIAL • PUNIC WAR SPECIAL

CARTHAGE

SECOND PUNIC WAR 218-201BC

ELEPHANT MAN IN MOUNTAIN BREAK OUT

218BC

Carthage is on the warpath and tough-guy Hannibal is at the helm! Since their defeat in the First Punic War, the Carts have taken over most of gold-and-silver-rich Spain. Now, following a rumpus with Rome over their occupation of **even more of it**, they're all set for a **full-scale ding-dong battle.**

Hannibal is reported to have sworn an oath of vengeance on the Romans. If he keeps

Jumbo trouble for Rome

going at this rate, we're all mincemeat. So far he's...
• Gathered together an army of hardened mercenaries from Spain and Africa.
• Obtained three dozen war elephants. Each one is equipped with **four huge stomping feet and two razor sharp tusks.**
• Taken the whole lot

of them and crossed over the mighty Alps. Inhospitable, craggy, snow-bound, ferocious – and that's just the savage tribes that are witless enough to live there, never mind the terrain itself.

Now he's in the Po valley in northern Italy – mere days away from Rome, and **Round Two of the Punic Wars is about to commence**. Please fasten your seat belts, spit out that chewing gum, and HOLD ON TIGHT!

"Cunc" does a bunk

217BC

Rome's military dictator, Quintus Fabius Maximus – (known as *Cunctator*, the delayer) has **again** refused to let our boys fight the Carthaginians. Quintus told the *Record*: "Hannibal is a military genius, and he'd love to take us on. But he's decided Rome's too well defended to attack directly, so he's trying to cut us off from the rest of the country.

"My policy is to let him flounder around Italy. History will prove me right, you'll see."

UN-PLEASANT UN-EDIFYING UN-CANNAE

216BC

Hot-head Romans have dismissed *Cunctator* Quint from his dictator job and ordered our legions to attack Hannibal. 86,000 soldiers, the largest army ever assembled in Roman history, met the Carthaginians at Cannae in the south of Italy. The result – **THE WORST DEFEAT EVER IN THE HISTORY OF OUR ROMAN CIVILIZATION.**

SO-AND-SO

"That Hannibal's a clever so-and-so," says Barracksus Brawlus, the *Record*'s military correspondent. "He's familiar with our tactics and knew we'd launch an all-out attack at his weakest point – the middle of his ranks of soldiers.

"So he put his best cavalry on his left and right wings, and when we did attack him in the middle he just encircled us. Our troops were so tightly packed in they didn't even have space to swing their swords. We've had 50,000 men killed and 10,000 taken prisoner. It's all a little upsetting."

Zama-wamma! Scipio wallops Carts

204BC

News is reaching the *Record* of a major Roman victory in Northern Africa.

Following our crushing defeat at Cannae, the army bosses realized that *Cunctator* Quint was correct, and let Hannibal flounder around in Italy for another thirteen years.

Meanwhile hot-shot Roman general Publius Cornelius Scipio invaded Carthaginian territory in Spain. Then he attacked North Africa.

Carthaginian army chiefs, correctly fearing for their safety, called back Hannibal to defend their city. Scipio clashed with Hannibal at the battle of Zama and beat him fair and square.

Peace negotiations are currently taking place, and Rome is expected to demand a **vast sum of money** (around 10,000 talents) and **no small amount of territory** (at least Spain) as compensation.

COLONIES ARE GIVING US INDIGESTION

No future? Some poor people hanging around in Rome, yesterday.

133BC

Burrrp! That's the state of Rome today. It's stuffed full of bloated citizens who've gobbled up too much territory.

Since the Punic Wars we've set up colonies all over the place – Carthage, Greece and Pergamum, to name just a few.

But some people are claiming that our new colonies are actually a BAD THING – especially if you're a peasant farmer.

This is what they're saying…

RUIN

•Peasant farmers, who made up most of the army, have spent so much of their time fighting, their farms are *overgrown and ruined*.

•Rich senators and businessmen have made *masses of money* from our conquests. They're spending it on buying up LAND from the poorer farmers, and creating huge farms worked by slaves brought in from conquered territories. Some politicians are even *swiping* land to give to their own soldiers as a reward for loyal service.

•The poorer farmers who have kept going, are being *forced out of business* by the big farms who can sell goods cheaper, and also by cheap food coming in from our new colonies.

FLOCK

•The poor farmers are flocking to the big cities – especially Rome – to look for work. But there are few jobs in the cities, because there are so many slaves to do them.

Our political correspondent Servius Sleazus II writes: This all adds up to a **really big problem**. These colonies have made a lot of money for a few rich people, and the rest of us are getting poorer. With Egypt to the south and Gaul to the north just **ripe** for conquest I predict **more** land-grabbing Empire building, and a **great deal of trouble and strife here in Rome.**

A big farm, yesterday. Social unrest not pictured.

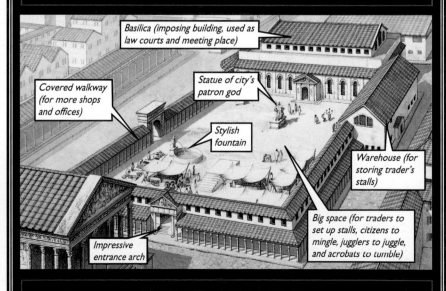

WHO'S TOPS WITH
OPS V. POPS?
OPTIMATES AND POPULARES CLASH

YOUR 10 POINT COUNTDOWN TO THE COLLAPSE OF THE REPUBLIC

59BC

Your *Record* is always right! We predicted stormy weather way back in 133BC and we were absolutely <u>on the button!</u> The richer and more successful we get, the more we're tearing ourselves apart. Now it looks like the Republic is about to collapse, and we're in for centuries of military dictatorship. The *Record* Countdown starts here....

10 In 133BC tribune Tiberius Gracchus proposes that some land owned by the VERY WEALTHY should be given to the VERY POOR. This ridiculous suggestion results in him and 300 of his supporters being **clubbed to death** by a **mob** led by land-owning senators.

9 In 123BC Gracchus's brother Gaius, also a tribune, initiates more land reforms. He and 3,000 of his supporters are **SEIZED AND KILLED**. The murder of the two brothers marks the end of political disagreements being settled by a nice chat, and the beginning of even more violence.

8 By 120BC two factions have emerged:
The Optimates – they say: We're all right Jack. Keep things as they are, and beat anyone who steps out of line with a big stick.
The Populares – they say: let's make things pleasanter for the poor by giving them more land to farm, and hand out grain to the starving.
After the slaying of the Gracchus brothers the *Optimates* have the upper hand.

7 107BC. The pendulum swings. Military campaigns led by *Optimates* go badly. Backlash results in election to consul of top *Popularis* General Marius. He defeats a bunch of foreigners and becomes even more popular.
However, he gets himself re-elected **six times in a row**, in direct defiance of Roman convention that consuls serve for one year only. Marius dominates Roman politics in a way **one man is not supposed to.**

6 88BC. Marius squabbles with Sulla – a consul, *Optimate*, and rising star. Sulla, with his own army in tow, marches on Rome to confront Marius. **Clear message to all *Record* Readers – If you thought an army was there to defend the state, YOU'RE COMPLETELY OUT OF DATE!!**

5 Marius flees and Sulla hops over to Asia to do some successful smiting and laying waste of King Mithradates of Pontus.
Rome collapses into rioting, assassinations, and all sorts of anarchy. Marius returns to restore order, kills any Sulla supporters he can find, and declares himself consul.

4 83BC. Marius dies of old age. Top *Optimate* Sulla returns to Rome and executes 6,000 *Populares* supporters of Marius. He is **declared dictator for as long as he wants the job.** (Previously, dictators only held office for six months during a dire emergency.) However, Sulla gets bored after four years, and retires to the country to write awful poetry.

3 70BC. Top soldier Pompey the Great takes a leaf out of Sulla's book, and turns **military success** abroad into **political popularity** at home. He is elected consul. Joining him at the top of the greasy political pole is fantastically wealthy land-owner Marcus Crassus.

2 61BC. Their pal Julius Caesar also becomes a **big noise** in Rome. Military genius, charismatic rabble rouser and top class brain, Caesar is blindingly brilliant, and almost too good to be true.

1 59BC. Cheesed off by the Senate's refusal to let them have their own way on everything they want, Pompey, Crassus and Caesar form the **First Triumvirate**, and arrange for Caesar to be elected consul. Roman politics reaches the stage where a few individuals are more powerful than the senate itself.

WARNING WARNING!!! BEEEP!!! BEEEEP!!! BRRRRRRRR RRINNGGG!!!

These men are about to trigger events which will topple 400 years worth of Roman Republic and bring about 500 years of military dictatorship. **STAND CLEAR!!!!**

JULIUS CAESAR

A NATION MOURNS

KNIFE-FIGHT WIPEOUT ENDS BRILLIANT CAREER

Remembered chiefly by the salad that was named after him, Caesar was the greatest man of his era.

44BC

Julius Caesar is dead – fatally stabbed by a gaggle of senators. His murder brings to an end the career of Rome's greatest soldier. He was 55.

Caesar was born into a posh patrician family in 100BC and went to the best schools in Rome and Rhodes. Always ambitious, he soon gained a reputation as a brilliant speaker, and rose quickly to the top in politics, siding with the *Populares*.

RAMPAGE

Palling up with fellow fat cats Pompey and Crassus, he took the job of consul in 59BC. His year as top man in Rome was followed by a nine year rampage through Gaul (that's France to our younger readers), which he added to the Empire. During his campaign, Caesar's troops blitzed a record-breaking, rampart-storming 800 towns! He also invaded Britain a couple of times, although he didn't stay.

OO-ER

But back in Rome his two allies Crassus and Pompey were having mixed fortunes. In 53BC Crassus went off to Asia to fight the Parthians. They completely wiped the floor with his army. AND his severed head was gleefully tossed at the feet of the Parthian king. (How embarrassing!)

Pompey had done better. Envious of Caesar's success he plotted with the senate (who were mostly *Optimates*) to bring Julius down a peg. In 52BC the senate declared Pompey sole consul and ordered Caesar to give up his army and come back to Rome.

Caesar sensed that returning home might well involve having **his** head tossed at *Pompey*'s feet. He came back to Rome, but sensibly took his army with him. So began a CIVIL WAR.

MURDER!

Caesar overran Italy, wiped out seven of Pompey's legions, and then chased him to Greece where he pulverized Pompey's army at Pharsalus. Pompey fled to Egypt, which was unwise. He was murdered the moment he stepped ashore, on the orders of a King anxious to keep on the right side of Caesar.

There followed a stopover in Egypt, where Caesar was presented with Pompey's embalmed head. He also found time to woo top local, Cleopatra, the dishiest queen in ancient history.

He returned to Rome in 46BC, and declared himself dictator for 10 years. Sensing they were thoroughly beaten, the senators nodded meekly.

PURPLE

Earlier **this year** he made himself dictator for life. He kept himself busy, giving land to 80,000 soldiers, reducing debts, improving the government, and commissioning some fine new buildings.

But many senators feared that power was going to his head. He rarely consulted the Senate, who had run Rome for the past 500 years. Senators thought he was acting like one of those kings they'd ousted in 510BC. He even appeared in public in a gilded chair, wearing a purple toga.

Fearing he was actually going to declare himself king, 60 senators attacked him during a political meeting, and stabbed him 23 times. (A strike rate of only slightly more than one senator in three – not very impressive.)

But the murder has not been greeted with much enthusiasm. Senators expecting to be applauded for their actions were greeted with stunned silence, and have fled to the hills.

The *Record* says: Watch this space for more edge-of-seat political high jinks!!!

7 THINGS YOU NEVER KNEW ABOUT CAESAR

★ The month of July is named after him.

★ The German and Russian words for king – Kaiser and Czar – are based on his name.

★ Caesar first met Cleopatra when she smuggled herself into his palace, wrapped in a carpet. Their red-hot romance held up the civil war for seven months!

★ Shortly afterward she had a son called Caesarion.

★ Caesar introduced a new 365-day calendar, which (give or take the odd tweak and extra day) is still in use today.

★ His daughter Julia was married to ally and then enemy Pompey. She died in childbirth shortly before the two men fell out.

★ He was elected chief of the Roman priesthood aged just 37 – an amazing feat, as the job always went to someone who was considerably wrinklier, and sage-like.

AN EMPIRE IS BORN!!

HOW SON OF CAESAR SEIZED CONTROL

Octavian, a.k.a Augustus, looking revered.

AD14

Welcome to the hottest series in history: the birth of the Roman Empire! After Caesar's murder there've been more twists and turns than a soap opera. So, for those of you who haven't been paying attention every week, HERE IS WHAT'S BEEN GOING ON...

CAST

MARK ANTONY

Caesar's dashing, handsome pal. Twinkle-eyed M.A. (as he's known to his friends) is a ladies' man from the top of his tousled black locks to the bottom of his dusty marching boots.

LEPIDUS

Caesar's second in command, and a dreary nonentity. Almost certain to be written out before we're halfway through.

OCTAVIAN

Caesar's steely 18 year-old nephew. He may be a callow student, but he's sharp as a razor!

CLEOPATRA

Queen of Egypt, femme fatale, and a real minx, by all accounts.

A cast of thousands of assorted legionaries, slaves, senators, dancing girls, armies, navies, and mobs with burning torches.

EPISODE ONE

Hearing his Uncle Caesar has declared him son and heir in his will, teenager Octavian hurries home from Athens University in Greece, to claim his inheritance. He learns that Mark Antony and Lepidus are after his job.

EPISODE TWO

Octavian leads an army against Mark Antony. He beats him, and then marches to Rome to demand a consulship – and all before he's 20. There's precocious!

EPISODE THREE

Consul Octavian meets with Mark Antony and Lepidus, and the three agree to rule Rome together. They have 45 legions between them, which adds up to a lot of soldiers to reward for their loyalty. The three draw up a list of 2,300 powerful enemies, have them executed, and divide their land and wealth between the troops. Ratings go sky high – especially with the execution scenes. We like that sort of thing in Rome.

EPISODE FOUR

Ructions at the top. Octavian and M.A. squabble over who does what, and almost come to blows. Octavian takes over the west of the Empire. Antony takes the east. Lepidus becomes increasingly irrelevant. Ratings drop. Spectators switch off in droves.

EPISODE FIVE

Lepidus turns on Octavian, but his troops desert him. He's such a wimp, Octavian doesn't even kill him. Meanwhile Mark Antony, who's based in Turkey, summons sultry Queen Cleopatra of Egypt to see him. She floats up to his doorstep wearing a gold-plated barge, and 19 gallons of exotic perfume. M.A.'s tongue hits the floor, and they return to Egypt together. The pitter patter of three pairs of tiny feet follow on. Ratings soar.

EPISODE SIX

Deliriously in love, M.A. starts handing out Roman territory to Cleo and their children. Octavian goes BALLISTIC.

EPISODE SEVEN

No-expense-spared showdown in Greece, as Mark Antony and Octavian clash in a thousand-ship sea battle at Actium. M.A. and Cleo are beaten and flee to Egypt, pursued by Octavian. In a shock double suicide, M.A. stabs himself in the stomach (very nasty) and Cleo has an elegant encounter with a poisonous asp. (Such style – and so like her.) Ratings go through ceiling!

EPISODE EIGHT

Octavian takes over the entire Empire, is declared supreme ruler and renamed Augustus – "the revered one". He is Rome's first Emperor. He halves the size of the army, and pays off his old troops with the riches he's gained from his various conquests. He also works closely with the senate, orders the construction of many wonderful buildings in Rome, and officially adds Egypt to the Empire. He is a great success for 45 years, and Rome prospers. By the time he dies, everyone accepts that one strong man will run the Empire, and **the idea of a republic is dead.**

TOUGHER
THAN THE REST

AD14

There's tough, there's tougher, then there's the Roman army. This week's IN FOCUS looks at what makes our boys in breastplates so world-beatingly great.

UNPOPULAR

Once, our army was a shambles. You could only join it if you owned property. You hardly ever got paid. And it was such an unpopular job that sometimes we had to enlist slaves just to keep the number up.

That's all changed. Now any citizen can join and our soldiers are full-time professionals who get a much better salary than the average worker.

What's more, a good war record carries major political clout if you're from the ruling class. Guess who's going to look most impressive in the Senate – Mr. Ploddus, dried-fish magnate from Ostia; or General Julius, heroic conqueror of Thrace and Segovia? No prize for the right answer!

POPULAR

So. The army's a Number One career choice for high and low alike. But can it deliver the goods? You bet! When it comes to battle capability we know no equal! We've got:
• State-of-the-art weaponry and training.
• Masses of soldiers (we're the biggest army in the world – stick that in your factfile, military buffs!)
• Streamlined organization.
• Fiendish discipline. Soldiers are flogged for the tiniest misdemeanours. As for mutiny or not fighting hard enough – well, any sign of that and we kill one in ten men as a warning to the others.

JOB

What are the retirement prospects? Plenty!! Having spent half your time learning how to build roads, towns and aqueducts, you'll never be at a loss for a job.

The *Record* says: ISN'T WARFARE WONDERFUL?

TOP GEAR

We invest in the best. The Roman army offers its soldiers the latest military technology.

❶ Scarf to stop breastplate from scratching neck.

❷ Wool cloak to make your neck itchy instead.

❸ Lightweight chain mail vest – doesn't keep out the cold, but useful for keeping out arrows.

❹ Wood/leather shield, with inlayed iron bands, for in-battle, peace-of-mind, extra protection.

❻ Hat with plume. Chic or what??!!

❼ Your everyday, whistle-while-you-work big sword.

❽ "Stealth" boots with extra-thick hob nail soles. Just what you need for those lightning-strike 30km (20 mile) route marches.

❾ Metal-tipped javelin. These can pierce chain mail, but if you miss, the soft iron tip bends on contact with the ground, so the enemy can't use it against you. Clever, eh?

WHO'S WHO IN THE ROMAN ARMY?

LEGIONARY

The sharp end of the army. He joins for 20 years, as part of a legion of around 5000 soldiers. He gets to see most of the known world. If he fights well and behaves himself, when he retires the army gives him a plot of land, or a cash bonus of 12 years pay.

CENTURION

He's in charge of a century – that's 80 men to you civilians. There are 60 centuries in a legion.

The centurion gets his own tent, whereas a legionary has to share with eight others – phooey – all those stinking feet!

SIGNIFIER

He carries the century's emblem into battle. He also runs a funeral club, to make sure soldiers get a proper burial if they're killed in battle. Now there's a comforting thought.

TRIBUNUS MILITUM

He's a junior officer, in charge of around 500 men. Look out for him – he's very ambitious.

LEGATUS

He's top man in the legion, and a friend of the Emperor. He won't know most of his troops from Adam, as there are 5,000 men under his command.

AQUILIFER

He carries the legion's standard – an eagle made of silver. If this is captured the legion is disbanded, and everyone is in **serious disgrace**.

AUXILIA

This bunch are non-citizens from our Empire. They get paid less, and can be a bit of a rabble. However, if they behave themselves they get to become Roman citizens when they leave the army after 20 years service.

MAD, BAD AND DANGEROUS TO KNOW!

WHO'S ROME'S MADDEST MR. MAD???

AD68

Emperors come and go. Sometimes we get lucky and sometimes we don't. Following the death of Augustus in AD14, we've had some of the most headbanging loony-tunes this side of a SPITTING COBRA. But who *is* the **maddest and, baddest?** READ ON…

	TIBERIUS AD14-37	CALIGULA AD37-41	CLAUDIUS AD41-54	NERO AD54-68
	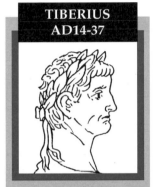			
WHO WAS HE?	Stepson of Augustus. Top soldier and pretty good at ruling. Strengthened frontiers of Empire, and saved up lots of money.	Great-nephew of Tiberius. Never quite right, even as a child. Got a lot worse once he became Emperor. Extremely extravagant – mainly with the money Tiberius had saved.	Nephew of Tiberius. Became Emperor at 50, having been plucked from obscurity by Palace guard following assassination of Caligula. Disabled, frail and nervous, he was far brighter than he looked.	Stepson of Claudius. Started off well, but power went to his head. Built a lot, including one of Rome's finest public baths, and a luxurious palace called the Golden House.
MAD?	Nope, but not unreasonable fear of assassination and unpleasant skin disease made him very edgy – not to mention rather unforgiving.	Built temple to himself, and appeared in it dressed as a goddess. Married sister. When she died he declared weeks of public mourning, when no one was allowed to laugh. Tried to have his horse declared consul. Assembled massive army to invade Britain, but forgot to provide ships for them to cross channel. Had them gather seashells instead.	Not remotely. Devoted his rule to improving the civil service, and involving the provinces more directly in government. He also added territory to the Empire. (Particularly Britain, and more of Greece.)	Artistic temperament – he thought the Greeks were wonderful and imagined himself as a poet, musician, charioteer and actor. When he performed NO ONE was allowed to leave the theatre, not even women to give birth. When he was really on form he had himself crowned five times a day.
BAD?	Not so much bad as hard to deal with. Moved from Rome to the remote isle of Capri, where he felt safer and ruled by post. Hit and miss nature of Roman postal service caused loss of patience in the capital, and prompted assassination attempts.	Told his girlfriends while kissing them on the neck, "You'll lose this beautiful head whenever I decide." The silver-tongued charmer! Alas, many of Caligula's activities are unsuitable for a family newspaper.	Not really. Main failing – a weakness for scheming wives, especially his fourth, Agrippina. (See below)	Blamed Christians for a great fire in Rome (AD64) and persecuted them mercilessly. Some were even tarred, staked and torched to provide illumination in his private gardens.
DANGEROUS TO KNOW?	Plots to depose him dealt with in starkly brutal fashion, and led to reign of terror in Rome, which cast long shadow over his final years as Emperor.	Usual executions of rivals and plotters against him. Had a courtier executed for being too well-groomed. Insisted the victim's father come to the execution, and then invited him to dinner.	Only if you wanted to kill him. Despite being good at his job, he lacked support of Rome's ruling class. Various assassination attempts resulted in execution of 35 senators during his reign.	Murdered mother, wife, brother, stepbrother, and forced tutor Seneca (the greatest philosopher of his age) to commit suicide. Also did away with scores more real and imagined rivals.
THEN WHAT?	He died of old age.	Assassinated by his own soldiers, and not a moment too soon.	Agrippina poisoned his mushroom soup to make way for her son Nero.	Committed suicide, shortly before his own soldiers came along to bump him off.

TRAJAN
TOPS THE LOT

Empire peaks at 100 million people

AD117

WE'RE BIGGER THAN EVER – AND THAT'S OFFICIAL! Emperor Trajan has captured large parts of the Middle East and Eastern Europe, and the Roman Empire is at its glowing, triumphant peak. You can walk from the frosty border of Britannia to the baking desert of Babylonia, and it's ALL OURS!!!

Mind you, a word of warning. Capturing a country isn't always sound business sense. We took over Britannia a hundred years ago, and it's proved to be a very poor investment. It costs far more in legionaries and the like to be there, than we ever get out of it. Still, never mind. Check out the map!! How do we do it? – See our special feature on page 13.

Some barbarians get the wrong side of our boys!

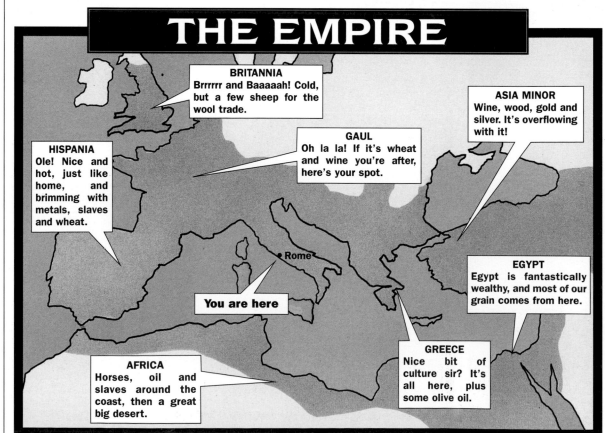

THE EMPIRE

BRITANNIA
Brrrrrr and Baaaaah! Cold, but a few sheep for the wool trade.

ASIA MINOR
Wine, wood, gold and silver. It's overflowing with it!

HISPANIA
Ole! Nice and hot, just like home, and brimming with metals, slaves and wheat.

GAUL
Oh la la! If it's wheat and wine you're after, here's your spot.

EGYPT
Egypt is fantastically wealthy, and most of our grain comes from here.

• Rome

You are here

GREECE
Nice bit of culture sir? It's all here, plus some olive oil.

AFRICA
Horses, oil and slaves around the coast, then a great big desert.

SMASH AND GRAB

Here's how we do it

YOUR NINE STEP GUIDE TO ACQUIRING A NEW COUNTRY

It all started with Sicily and Spain. Now look where we've ended up! But how **do** we go about adding to our Empire? Follow this nine-step guide, and you can't go wrong.

❶ Pick a country on our border with something in it worth stealing (Wheat, sheep, wine, silver, we're not fussy). If the tribes there are a threat to Rome, so much the better. If you conquer them, all the more glory for YOU!

❷ Invade it with our large, extremely disciplined and ferociously unpleasant army (see page 10).

❸ Pick on a few towns and raze them to the ground, killing everything that moves inside them. (This lets the locals know we really mean business.)

❹ Charge them an *indemnity* – a fine imposed on all newly conquered peoples to cover the expense of fighting them.

❺ Build some roads. These let us move troops around to crush rebellions very quickly. What's more, a messenger can travel 80km (50 miles) a day on a Roman road. Who needs to invent the telephone!

❻ Establish some towns. They don't really have these in western Europe (although the eastern side of the Empire is well acquainted with urban life). Towns are beacons in a dark mist of barbarity. Their fine civic buildings, baths, aqueducts and amphitheatres can't fail to impress the locals, who don't really stretch to anything more than a few mud huts and rickety rope bridges.

❼ Are there any local top dogs around who we didn't kill when we conquered the place? Get them to run the towns. They'll soon see it's in their interests to keep everyone sweet. Reward them with Roman citizenship if they're good.

❽ Respect the local religion and customs if they're not a threat to Rome. After all, we don't want any needless aggravation over something silly like wearing a braided beard, stone worship, or sacrificing a couple of maidens every spring.

❾ Make sure our frontiers are secure by building a big wall, or a ditch at the very least.

If we've played our cards right, we'll be able to get the locals to defend it, especially if we pay them well.

Attention all conquered territories! Once we've got the nasty business of defeating you out of the way, this is what your country could look like. Nice, isn't it!

WALL MAN BACKS DOWN

HADRIAN CALLS A HALT

AD130

Frostius Breechus, your Edge of Empire correspondent, shivering to death on the outer limits of Britannia, sends this report from the River Tyne.

Here I stand neck-deep in cold, damp fog. It's not difficult to see why Emperor Hadrian has chosen this spot to mark the most northerly extent of the Roman Empire. It's a barren wasteland, and farther north are tribes of untameable barbarians, not to mention the odd dragon and packs of ferocious three-headed dogs with very big teeth.

RAMPART

The wall here combines good old-fashioned Roman grit and determination with the very latest in rampart technology. It's been built in just seven years by the Roman army, and stretches an uninterrupted 130km (80 miles) across the width of this country.

NAIL

It's a clear message to the barbarian Picts and Scots who live on the other side. It says "We're extremely well organized and efficient, and if you come over looking for trouble we'll nail your ears to the floor."

ENOUGH

With frontiers in Germany, along the Danube, and down in the east, Hadrian has decided that we've conquered about as much territory as we can hold on to. And that's good news for Rome, and good news for the Roman Empire.

Hadrian's very own out-on-the-edge wall. Not a popular army posting.

CALAMITY CLAIM
CAUSES CONCERN

IS FUTURE BLEAK???

AD235

We know we're the greatest civilization on Earth, after all WE'VE GOT A MASSIVE EMPIRE TO PROVE IT. But they say pride comes before a fall, and according to a soothsayer's report commissioned by the *Record*, THAT might well be the fall of the Roman Empire! Our team of top entrail dabblers say:

• We're becoming too complacent for our own good.

• We've gone from being tough guys to nerds who complain if our orgies aren't disgusting enough.

• The future looks greedy, brutal, corrupt and incompentent.

• That'll be 500 denarii, please.

HOPELESS

The Record blames the men at the top. Since AD180 we've been saddled with a succession of sometimes hopeless, fly-by-night Emperors, just when we needed **some good men for the job.** (Check out our **Who was who** guide to Rome's most recent rulers, right.)

But hard-line Senator Whackus Maximus disagrees with our forecast. He told the *Record*: "Any talk about the fall of the

Empire is just drivel. Just wander around the dazzling metropolis of Rome, then wonder at the roads and aqueducts we've built from Britannia to Egypt, and you can see that. D'you know we can trade from Spain to Syria and they'll accept our Roman money? **We're as safe as houses!**"

Some concerned soothsayers. Politicians have dismissed their report as "drivel".

WHO WAS WHO?

EMPERORS WHO CAME AND WENT

AD180-235

Commodus AD180-192

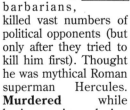

Made peace with invading barbarians, killed vast numbers of political opponents (but only after they tried to kill him first). Thought he was mythical Roman superman Hercules. **Murdered** while having a nice relaxing soak in the bath.

Pertinax AD192

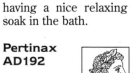

Not very interesting. **Murdered.**

Septimius Severus AD193-211

Introduced taxation of Roman citizens to help pay for vast cost of defending Empire. Came from Africa and spoke Latin with funny accent, which he never lost.

Had terrible temper, but this is not surprising, as he spent half of time on throne fighting off rivals. Had some success restoring peace and order to the Empire, and held on to his job for an admirably long time.

Reformed justice system to give poor a better deal. **Died** at York, in Britain, after successful but exhausting campaign against invading Picts from Scotland. Left Empire to two sons – Caracalla and Geta.

Caracalla AD211-217

Killed brother and (allegedly) 20,000 other rivals for throne. Raised army pay, bribed barbarians to stay away from borders, granted citizenship to all free males in Empire, but only so he could tax them. Idolized Greek supremo Alexander the Great, and planned massive conquest of East. **Murdered.**

Macrinus AD217-218

Murderer of Caracalla. **Deposed.**

Elagabalus AD218-222

Despotic, pimply youth, who was fanatically dedicated to the worship of some obscure Syrian sun-god. **Murdered.**

Severus Alexander AD222-235

More like it. Became Emperor at rather precocious age of 13, so his mother Julia ruled for him. She made sure the army behaved itself, and let some powerful senators look after the Empire.

Improved life for the lowly, with hand-outs for teachers and scholars, and landlords who repaired their properties.

However, he failed to deal with barbarian threat to Empire in north, so mother and son both **murdered.**

God-Man Dio Goes For Glory

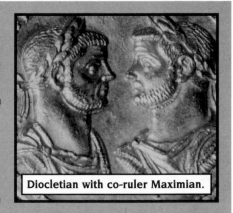

Diocletian with co-ruler Maximian.

AD305

What's that clacking sound? Is it castanets? Nope. That's our teeth rattling as Emperor Diocletian grabs the Empire by the scruff of the neck and shakes some life into it.

Strong Man Dio, formerly a peasant from Dalmatia, has launched a series of shock reforms in a last minute attempt to avert catastrophe. Here's what he's done so far...

DIO'S DOINGS

• He's clamped down on tax dodgers. Extra revenue gained pays for improving and enlarging the army, so we can defend our Empire better.
• He's claimed he's top god Jupiter's agent on Earth, which means that Dio's almost a god himself. Not only that, but he insists on being addressed as 'Your Majesty', wears snazzy purple and gold robes, and demands that everyone kiss the hem of his robe when they see him. ("It's not for me," he insists. "It's to bring back respect for the tarnished office of Emperor.")
• He's tried to tackle runaway inflation by freezing prices on everything from bread and salt to hare's fur underwear and fattened goldfinch snacks.
• He's introduced an annual budget for his government, so that provincial governors will know in advance how much tax to raise.
• He's mercilessly persecuting Christians "What's

wrong with the old gods, that's what I say," he told the *Record*. "I like conformity and obedience, and these Christians are a bad influence."

AND MOST IMPORTANT OF ALL...
• He's split the Empire into two parts – East and West. He says it's too big, and two Emperors working together with two governments will make it easier to control. He's appointed fellow big wig Maximian to look after the West while he looks after the East.

TRUCK

Diocletian has been quick to defend his controversial reforms. "Desperate times demand desperate measures. When I came to power it was anarchy. Between 235 and 284 we had 18 Emperors in less than 50 years, money all but lost its value, and our economy fell into ruins. Instead of working the farms, peasants were fleeing to the cities, or turning bandit. The Empire was falling to pieces. I said to myself, 'there's life in the old dog yet,' and d'you know, **I was right**."

IT'S CAPITAL!!

Constantinople is Empire's number one city

AD330

Emperor Constantine has made an epic bid for immortality. He's already made a massive mark on the world by officially ending the Roman persecution of Christians, leaving the way open for Christianity to become the Empire's top religion. Now he's founded a new capital for the eastern part of the Empire, and named it after **himself**.

SEEDY

Constantine told the *Record*. "Rome's become a bit seedy lately. Besides, the eastern side of the Empire is a

Constantine shows his pals a model of Constantinople.

lot more stable and prosperous than the west, so it makes sense to run things from here. The old Greek city of Byzantium is well placed for trade, and is very well defended. **So we're launching a massive building project, and renaming it after me**.

HIPPO

"Architects have been summoned from all over the Empire to build prestigious city buildings, such as a hippodrome, forum and senate house. Statues and treasure from Rome, Athens and anywhere else that's got any, are also being transferred here.

"It's time to turn over a new leaf. Rome's washed out. It's pagan, and rooted

in the past. Constantinople stands for everything that's fresh about the Empire. We're mainly Christian, most of us speak Greek, and we intend to be a beacon for the civilized world for a thousand years to come."

CRUMBLE

But critics say the foundation of the city will further hasten the decline of the Empire. By taking power and wealth from Rome, it leaves the western half of the crumbling Empire vulnerable to barbarian hordes massing on the borders. (See page 16 for the latest news on THEM.)

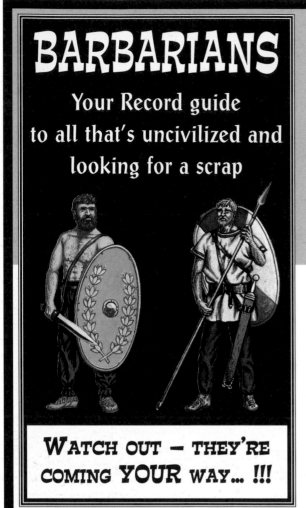

BARBARIANS

Your Record guide to all that's uncivilized and looking for a scrap

WATCH OUT – THEY'RE COMING YOUR WAY... !!!

I MAGINE THE SCENE. YOU'RE SITTING IN YOUR VILLA ENJOYING A LEISURELY BREAKFAST OF BAKED FLAMINGO TONGUES. SUDDENLY A HUGE HAIRY FELLOW WITH A FUNNY HELMET AND A BIG AXE POKES HIS HEAD THROUGH THE WINDOW AND BELLOWS SOMETHING OBSCENE. WHAT DO YOU DO, PAT HIM ON THE HEAD OR RUN LIKE MAD? READ OUR GUIDE AND FIND OUT!

GOTH

Habitat: *Europe, Western Russia*

Most prominent of all barbarians. Species can be found in various forms throughout Europe, with much individual variation. Natural enemy of Vandal and Hun. Big, beardy, long-haired types who like a fight and can drink beer for days without falling over. Generally recognizable by broad physique, round shield, short sword, and dog-like obedience to chief.

Distinctive feature:
Most of them have one of these.

OSTROGOTH

Habitat: *Western Russia.*

Type of Goth. Can walk naked through snow storms. Eats grass and roots. Despite hard-as-nails reputation, have recently been crushed by Huns.

Distinctive feature:
They like to wave these around.

VISIGOTH

Habitat: *Eastern Europe*

Yet another species of Goth. Semi-tame, but liable to turn nasty if over-taxed by greedy officials, and generally treated with contempt. Spitting, swearing types, and rather vulgar, so watch your step.

Distinctive feature:
Lots of them have reddish-blond hair.

GAUL

Habitat: *France and parts of Belgium*

This Celtic species can be fairly tame and cooperative, but is prone to occasional revolts. However, if treated with respect, a Gaul will repay you with loyalty and devotion.

Distinctive feature:
Nifty little chain-mail tunic.

SAXON

Habitat: *Coastal Northern Europe*

Voracious predator, eager to migrate to Gaul and Britannia. Skilled in piracy. Has worst table manners this side of frenzied Tyrannosaurus. Avoid if possible.

Distinctive feature:
Their heavy axes are a serious health hazard.

FRANK

Habitat: *Lower Rhine*

Leaner and swarthier than most other species. Has characteristic shaved back of head, with rest of hair gathered in fetching "top-knot". Natural enemy of Gauls. Quite dangerous when provoked. Usually fights on foot without helmet or other body protection. Prominent weapons – small throwing axe, javelin and short sword.

Distinctive feature:
Nice, bright striped wool tunic.

HUN

Habitat: *Eurasian plains*

Smallest of all barbarians. Feared foes of Goths and Vandals, ferocious warrior nomads and frighteningly efficient archers. Other barbarians running away from this bunch are spilling into OUR TERRITORY and causing no end of problems.

Has prominent and sinister ritual scarring on face, and always fights on horseback. Voted all time winners of annual *Gut-wrenchingly-terrifying-foe-we-would-least-like-to-fight* competition in *Roman Soldier Monthly*. Dour in appearance. Lives on diet of baked babies and tree bark gnawed straight from branch. Also reported to wear shrunken human heads as earrings, and smell worse than a beached whale.

If encountered, remain very still and hope they don't spot you. If contact unavoidable, do not attempt to engage in conversation, especially regarding relative merits of Greek or Roman poetry. Approach with extreme caution carrying long spear, and toss over some raw meat on end of a stick.

Distinctive feature:
Absolutely lethal with a bow and arrow.

VANDAL

Habitat: *Hungary*

All too common these days. Nomadic species and fiercely predatory. Guaranteed to smash up any form of public transportation, and carve name on park benches. Enemy of Visigoths, and dedicated to erasure of Roman culture.

Distinctive feature:
None: Look pretty much the same as the others.

BRITON

Habitat: *British Isles*

Usually harmless. Similar to Gaul, but habitat more inhospitable. Watch out for Picts and Scots branch of species in north of the Island.

Distinctive feature:
None worth mentioning.

SASSANID

Habitat: *Persia*

Treacherous, and thriving in east of Empire. Disappointingly civilized for barbarians. If encountered is more likely to discuss supremacy of Sassanid architecture over Roman, than flay you alive over snake pit. Caution: Still very dangerous and acquisitive.

Distinctive feature:
Great helmets! They obviously like a joke!

ROMAN RECORD DISCLAIMER
Some of these illustrations are based on very rare sightings, so we cannot guarantee their accuracy.

ROME RANSACKED BY RAMPAGING GOTHS

WAAAAAGH! THEY'RE HEEEERE!!

AD410

Never mind "The barbarians are at the gates" – the barbarians are INSIDE the Empire's most famous city, AND THEY'RE LOOTING ROME LIKE THERE'S NO TOMORROW!!!

Eyewitnesses say that anything that isn't nailed down or too heavy to lift is being loaded onto carts and horses and driven away. AND WHAT'S MORE, THERE'S NOTHING WE CAN DO ABOUT IT.

OH DEAR

It's been downhill all the way since Constantine died in AD337. The usual squabbles and civil wars occurred over his successor. Then we dithered about, wondering whether to be Pagans or Christians. While all this was going on, no one noticed the barbarians were really getting themselves organized.

By the time they invaded the Empire in AD378 and beat one of our armies at Adrianople, it was too late to complain. We were too weak to kick them out, so we made treaties with them and got them to work on our farms and in our army.

BUNCH

But in AD402 a bunch of Goths led by Alaric INVADED Italy itself, and now they've even occupied Rome. Fortunately Emperor Honorius moved his Imperial court from Rome in AD402, and made Ravenna the capital of the Western half of the Empire. But Rome hasn't been knocked about like this since it was sacked by Gauls nearly 800 years ago, **so it's still a terrible blow.**

In the last year alone Spain has been invaded and overrun by Vandals, AND we've had to abandon Britain. Disease and famine are sweeping through the population. **The *Record* says:**
WE'RE HANGING ON BY OUR FINGER-NAILS...

Plenty of looting, but no fiddling. Rome burning, yesterday.

Exploding Brain Kills

Honeymoon Hun

BEDROOM CATASTROPHE FOR ATTILA THE KILLER

Attila, heading for a disappointing honeymoon.

AD453

Top Hun Attila "the Hun" kissed his bride Ildeco goodnight, then dropped dead! Blond, buxom Ildeco, a German princess, told the *Record*: "Instead of whispering sweet nothings in my ear he said "I've got a headache." Some headache that turned out to be! A blood vessel in his brain burst and it was over and out before you could say donner und blitzen!"

SMIRK

The news is sure to bring a smirk to the face of Roman soldiers everywhere. Newlywed Attila, formidable leader of Rome's most feared foes, has terrorized the Empire for 10 years.

Half-beast mongol horsemen, the Huns were Rome's one-time allies, and helped us keep other barbarians in order. But their successes against various assorted Alans, Visigoths, Ostrogoths and Burgundians **went to their heads.**

Attila decided that the smart money lay in attacking the Empire itself, rather than a rag-tag assortment of peripheral barbarians. The wily head Hun has:

•**Laid waste** the Balkans in AD443 and headed for Constantinople, only turning back when petrified city bosses gave him a golden handshake of 2,750kg (6,000lb) of gold.

•**Came back** to Constantinople in AD447 anyway, defeating a Roman army en route, and demanded another MASSIVE handout to go away.

•**Invaded** Gaul in AD451 with a mighty army of barbarian allies, and fought an enormous Roman army to a stalemate at the battle of Troyes.

OH NO!
IT'S ODOACER!!

"MY BARBARIAN SHAME" BY EMPEROR AUGUSTULUS

"Hi, I'm a Vandal, and I've come to loot and pillage the Roman Empire like there's no tomorrow. Have a nice day now, and mind how you go."

AD476

Emperor Romulus Augustulus has spoken for the first time about his deposition by barbarian chief Odoacer. Safe in exile in a snug provincial castle in Naples, he spoke exclusively to the *Record*'s political correspondent Servius Sleazus IV.

Servius. So what's happened to your job then?

Augustulus. From what they tell me, after we fought Attila to a stalemate in 451, there were the usual squabbles about who was going to be Emperor. Meanwhile, various barbarians took over our territory in Spain, Africa, and Gaul. Then this Goth fellow, Odoacer, comes along to Ravenna where I was having a turn at being Emperor, and tells me to pack my bags and head as far south as possible. Then he said he was going to be King of Italy. And bingo, that was that – the end of the Roman Empire – or at least the western half of it.

S. So how do you feel about the fact that you weren't executed? Odoacer obviously doesn't see you as much of a threat.

A. Well, in some ways it's quite an insult. I'm the last ruler in a line of nearly 500 years worth of *Emperors, and you'd think he'd have had me strangled or something – just to mark the magnitude of the occasion. But between you and me, the sun is shining, there's a roast pig on the spit, a gallon of cooled wine in the cellar, and I'm quite glad to be alive really.*

S. And do you have a message for the citizens of the Empire who now face a life of barbarian discomfort, the prospect of watching their running water tail off to a trickle, and their temples get choked with weeds?

A. *I do. It's "That's all, folks. No refunds are available."*

CONSTANTINOPLE
IS OH SO PRETTY

AD500

It's not all doom and gloom in the Roman Empire. We may be sitting in the ruins of a crumbling civilization here in Rome, but the eastern territories around Constantinople are still sitting pretty. If you're looking for that fast-fading Roman way of life, then get on the next boat out there!

What have they got? A stable Roman-style government and army, Christian religion, and a fantastic chariot racing stadium at Constantinople (complete with all the usual modern conveniences), that's what!

HORDES

As the western half of the Empire has declined, so the east has grown richer. How's that?
• Far fewer hordes of barbarians invading them.
• They've had the good sense to talk their way into a settlement with their greatest enemy, the Persians.
• Far fewer Emperors, who usually stay in power a lot longer than ours

have done in the west. And they usually rule well. Their current Emperor, Anastasius, is balancing his budgets and even cutting taxes.

PERCH

And what's more, their main city, Constantinople, is perched right on the crossroads of Europe and Asia. It's in a perfect spot for trade, and is all set to become powerful and immensely wealthy. Our business correspondent Lunchus Accountus says:
The West may have collapsed, but in the East they've got enough to keep them going for another thousand years.

In the next 50 years we'll become so prosperous we'll be able to build churches like this.

REMEMBER US THIS WAY

WE SAY THERE'S MORE TO US ROMANS THAN LION FEEDING, EMPEROR KILLING AND SLAVERY.

With all this mayhem going on, and the world collapsing around our ears, it's about time we had something positive to say about ourselves. We were smart enough to get a lot of our ideas from the Greeks. (See our special report on page 28.) But what have we given the world? Read on...

LATIN for a start. For almost two thousand years, the language of science, law, medicine and diplomacy will be Latin, and anyone who wants to get along in the world will have to learn it.

Not only that but French, Spanish, Portuguese, Italian and Romanian will all become languages directly based on Latin. Even English will have at least 12,000 words that come from Latin.

CITIES. Most of western Europe had no cities before we came along. We founded such great cities as London, Paris, Lyon, Cologne, Milan and countless smaller towns and settlements. We didn't build New York, but it's streets are directly based on our grid system.

Our **BUILDINGS**. With their elegant arches, domes and concrete construction, people will still be copying our buildings in 1500 years' time. Famous generals like Napoleon, and Frederick the Great of Prussia, will build triumphal arches just like ours to celebrate great victories. Even United States President Thomas Jefferson will base his government buildings in Washington on ours. (Their government will even have senators and a senate!)

Our **LEGAL SYSTEM.** Six massive volumes of our statutes, decisions and commentaries will be incorporated into the laws of Church and Medieval courts in Europe, and become part of legal systems throughout the world.

THE GREEKS. People will know about Greek writing and art because we preserved and copied it. What we did will survive, whereas most of the original Greek versions won't.

And that's just a slice of what we've given to the world. Our ideas for government and empire, politics and philosophy, painting and sculptures, plays and poetry (some fellow called Shakespeare will take a lot of his plots from Roman stories, for example), will all be copied, and influence the way the world is run for thousands of years into the future.

EDITORIAL

WHY THE END IS NIGH

AD500

SO WHAT'S IT ALL ABOUT THEN, THIS FALL OF THE ROMAN EMPIRE?

It's not difficult to see how we rose from being a bolshie little city to rulers of Western Europe and the entire Mediterranean. The fact that a lot of our opponents were declining old empires or disorganized rabbles obviously helped. But we had a fair few fights on our hands too – especially with that Hannibal.

WELL

We did so well because we were the best. Having the most ruthless and determined army was a major advantage. But having the best roads, and the best planned towns and cities didn't go amiss. We also had a system of government that encouraged Empire building by rewarding successful generals with political power. AND we had the good sense to let the people we conquered become citizens of our Empire. Some even rose to become Emperor!

WATER

Why it all fell apart is a lot more complicated. There are several theories around, and none of them hold much water. Some say we lost our will to fight when we adopted kindly, merciful Christian values. This doesn't explain why the Eastern Empire – which was far more thoroughly Christian – continues to thrive. Others say we got too fat and flabby with *our appalling amphitheatres* and slaves and alley cat morals. But they were saying stuff like that in 200BC, and that was 700 years ago.

MARBLES

Another theory goes that many of our leaders got brain damage after drinking water that had too much lead in it. (This got into the supply from lead pipes used to transport water to our cities.) This doesn't stand up either. We use clay pipes wherever possible, and drink very little lead-piped water.

WONDER

So what is it that's caused the collapse of such a monumental Empire? The *Record* says the wonder is that we've lasted so long, not that we've finally collapsed.

With an Empire and culture stretching 16,000km (10,000 miles) from Britain to the Caspian Sea it was bound to be vulnerable to attack. We fought off invasions for 200 years. But when the cost of defending our frontiers from hoards of barbarians became too great, our Empire collapsed like a deck of cards.

ROME

THE OUT-OF-TOWNER'S GUIDE TO THE WORLD'S

No.1 CITY!

ETERNAL CITY OR FLESHPOT CESSPOOL???

THEATRE OF MARCELLUS

THE CIRCUS MAXIMUS

Parades. We like a parade. When one of our Emperors wins a big battle he marches through the city with his troops and captives and booty. The troops hurl insults at him (it's considered good luck) and everyone else cheers and throws flowers. Then the captives are strangled or sold as slaves, and everyone has a big feast.

AD100

Okay. You've made a little money in Britannia or Gaul, and now you want to SPEND IT. Or maybe you're a poor carpenter from Ravenna who wants to make his fortune in the big city. Where better to go than ROME? Grander than Mount Olympus. More beautiful than Venus. More zing than one of Jupiter's thunderbolts. A glittering whirlpool of power, corruption, and crazy, crazy people – that's Rome. And what's more – all roads lead to it.

But be careful. Your wildest dreams could turn into your worst nightmares. When you visit Rome you're putting your head in the lion's mouth. It might just get bitten off!

ROME FACTS

We may have copied a lot of our architecture from the Greeks, but Rome makes Greek cities like Athens look like a provincial horse and cart station. Check out these Rome facts:

One MILLION Romans make this the biggest city in the world, and 400,000 of them are slaves! That means most of the other 600,000 of them get to sit on their fat behinds a lot, and bellow for more WINE and ENTERTAINMENT, especially when it's one of the city's 100 annual feast days.

Fortune tellers say there won't be a European city this big again until Nineteenth century London.

Nineteen stone aqueducts keep those thirsty, dirty Romans supplied with constant fresh water.

LOOK AT THIS LOT!

Every Emperor wants to be remembered forever, and what better way than by ordering the construction of one of the most spectacular buildings in the world.

Temples, public baths, theatres, ornamental gardens, race tracks. Take your pick, we've got THE BEST.

THE CIRCUS MAXIMUS

Maximus thrills and spills at the chariot racetrack with the highest death rate in the city. Room for 200,000 inside.

THEATRE OF MARCELLUS

We like a little culture too, you know. It's not just chariot races and gladiators here.

BATHS OF TRAJAN

Just one of the city's 11 public baths. Lollop in the hot pool. Shiver in the

FORUM OF AUGUSTUS

Basilica. No, not a type of plant, but a public building used as a law court or government office. Plenty of these in Rome.

Statues, we got THOUSANDS of 'em! This one was built by mad-cap Emperor Nero, as a likeness of himself. When he was assassinated they lopped the head off, and replaced it with Apollo the sun god.

BATHS OF TRAJAN

THE COLOSSEUM

AQUEDUCT OF NERO

Arch. (See Parades). When an Emperor wins a battle he builds one of these to show how wonderful he is. Then he and his soldiers march under it.

Temple of the Divine Claudius. Rome has so many temples it's easy to get blasé about them. This one's quite nice though, with its gardens and everything.

TOP TIPS FOR TOURISTS

They say when in Rome do as the Romans do, so here's what you have to do to avoid standing out like the straw-chewing bumpkin you actually are...

WHEELS

Anything with wheels on is BANNED during the day. You can only bring your horse and cart into the city at night, and it's almost gridlock even then.

LITTER

If you can afford it, get yourself carried around in a litter, so you won't have to walk in the mud and sewage that coats the pavement. You can also look down on all the beggars, drunks, thieves and peddlers that will see you as EASY PREY if you're on their level.

WASTE

Try and avoid the narrowest streets. They're uncomfortably crowded AND people throw their waste out of windows. If you do get drenched by the contents of a chamber pot, just feel lucky it wasn't a brick or concrete beam. Plenty of them fall off the tops of buildings every day.

FERRETS

If you must go out at night, DO take some bodyguards. As well as ferrety bottom-of-the-heap poor people, who'll rob tourists like you quicker than you can say *Tempus fugit*, there are also gangs of posh kids, who think it's fun to go out and give an unsuspecting passer-by a good kicking.

cold pool. Wander in the cool shade of the ornamental gardens. Watch a boxing or wrestling match.

AQUEDUCT OF NERO

He may have been mad, bad and dangerous to know, but Emperor Nero did make himself useful by building this aqueduct to carry water from the countryside into the city.

THE COLOSSEUM

50,000 can cram in here to witness the most degrading, disgusting, deplorable spectacles money can buy. See Gladiators fight to the death in their thousands! (Frankly, it gets boring after the first ten or eleven.) See the senseless slaughter of wild and exotic animals on the very brink of extinction! See Christians being fed to the lions! **Sounds great doesn't it?** But it gets better – it's absolutely **FREE!!**

FORUM OF AUGUSTUS

Stuffed with temples and law courts. Emperor Augustus turned Rome from shoddy bricks to gleaming marble, and this forum is one of his many building projects. Most cities have one forum, Rome has at least three.

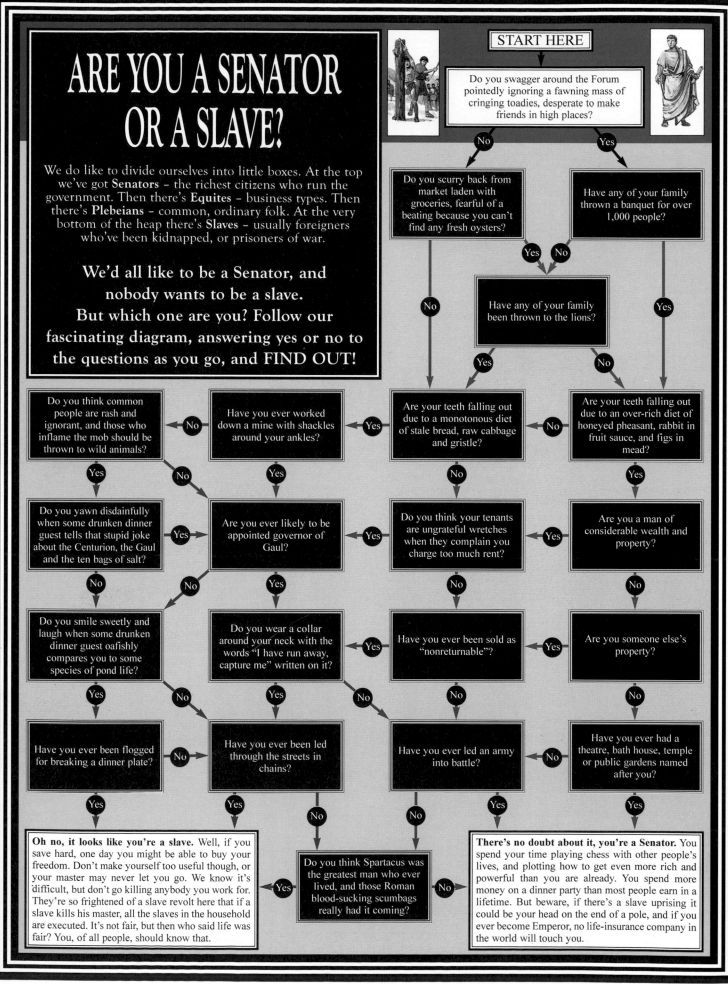

ARE YOU A SENATOR OR A SLAVE?

We do like to divide ourselves into little boxes. At the top we've got **Senators** - the richest citizens who run the government. Then there's **Equites** - business types. Then there's **Plebeians** - common, ordinary folk. At the very bottom of the heap there's **Slaves** - usually foreigners who've been kidnapped, or prisoners of war.

We'd all like to be a Senator, and nobody wants to be a slave. But which one are you? Follow our fascinating diagram, answering yes or no to the questions as you go, and FIND OUT!

START HERE

Do you swagger around the Forum pointedly ignoring a fawning mass of cringing toadies, desperate to make friends in high places?

No — Do you scurry back from market laden with groceries, fearful of a beating because you can't find any fresh oysters?

Yes — Have any of your family thrown a banquet for over 1,000 people?

Have any of your family been thrown to the lions?

Are your teeth falling out due to a monotonous diet of stale bread, raw cabbage and gristle?

Are your teeth falling out due to an over-rich diet of honeyed pheasant, rabbit in fruit sauce, and figs in mead?

Do you think common people are rash and ignorant, and those who inflame the mob should be thrown to wild animals?

Have you ever worked down a mine with shackles around your ankles?

Do you think your tenants are ungrateful wretches when they complain you charge too much rent?

Are you a man of considerable wealth and property?

Do you yawn disdainfully when some drunken dinner guest tells that stupid joke about the Centurion, the Gaul and the ten bags of salt?

Are you ever likely to be appointed governor of Gaul?

Do you smile sweetly and laugh when some drunken dinner guest oafishly compares you to some species of pond life?

Do you wear a collar around your neck with the words "I have run away, capture me" written on it?

Have you ever been sold as "nonreturnable"?

Are you someone else's property?

Have you ever been flogged for breaking a dinner plate?

Have you ever been led through the streets in chains?

Have you ever led an army into battle?

Have you ever had a theatre, bath house, temple or public gardens named after you?

Oh no, it looks like you're a slave. Well, if you save hard, one day you might be able to buy your freedom. Don't make yourself too useful though, or your master may never let you go. We know it's difficult, but don't go killing anybody you work for. They're so frightened of a slave revolt here that if a slave kills his master, all the slaves in the household are executed. It's not fair, but then who said life was fair? You, of all people, should know that.

Do you think Spartacus was the greatest man who ever lived, and those Roman blood-sucking scumbags really had it coming?

There's no doubt about it, you're a Senator. You spend your time playing chess with other people's lives, and plotting how to get even more rich and powerful than you are already. You spend more money on a dinner party than most people earn in a lifetime. But beware, if there's a slave uprising it could be your head on the end of a pole, and if you ever become Emperor, no life-insurance company in the world will touch you.

PEER INTO THE MISTY REALMS OF TOMORROW WITH THE ROMAN RECORD

Watching the sky

16 ancient sages in Rome called augers peer at the sky. Then they make predictions based on the shapes of flocks of birds, clouds and lightning. This is the most ancient divination technique known to Romans.

What they said to Bibulous:
"The conjugation of a dark thundercloud, and the hooting of an owl in the east at sunset, quite clearly suggests that the gods will visit an adverse foreign exchange rate on this business venture."

Pros
Venerable, respected, sanctioned by tradition.

Cons
They could say ANYTHING, couldn't they?

FORETELLING THE FUTURE

Let's face it, who WOULDN'T like to know what the future holds in store? But with so many different ways of predicting the will of the gods, which one <u>do</u> you go for? All of the methods we currently use go in and out of fashion as much as the cut of your tunic. And all of them are so old we've forgotten why they work and even where they came from.

WE'VE GONE CRITICAL

Here at the *Record* we thought it was about time we turned a critical eye on the prediction industry. So when businessman Bibulous Unctuous wrote to us recently asking whether he should invest in the Armenian slave trade we put our top divination techniques to the test.

We've picked five of the most well known, and asked their practitioners whether the gods would look aimiably on Bibulous's investment. Here's what they said, followed by what WE think about it.

Our verdict: There's a sucker born every minute!

The sibylline books

These are a set of prophesies by the prophetess Sibyl who lived in a cave near Naples around 750BC.

They're kept in the Temple of Apollo in Rome and, following authorization by the Senate, are consulted by seers at times of extreme national crisis.

What they said to Bibulous:
"Whether you should invest in the Armenian slave trade is NOT what WE would consider an EXTREME NATIONAL CRISIS. Now be off with you, and don't show your face here again.

Pros
Nice walk up to the temple.

Cons
Crotchety staff. No prediction.

Palm reading

Some old lady looks at the lines on your palm and makes predictions based on them.

What she said to Bibulous:
"The broken lifeline in the mount of Venus suggests you will soon be run over by a chariot while crossing the road, and therefore will be unable to enjoy any adequate return on your investment."

Pros
Dramatic increase in road-safety drill for Bibulous.

Cons
Reply limited only by palm-reader's imagination.

Animal innards

A special priest called a haruspice slits open a sacrificial animal and examines its liver. Then he makes predictions about the gods' attitude to your special problem, according to whether the liver's the wrong shape, or blotchy, or the right shape and clear.

He also pronounces on weeping statues and talking cows.

What he said to Bibulous:
"Well, this oddly bulbous vein here is a clear indicator that the gods are partial to low returns on your immediate investment. However, the slightly grey tinge to the upper lobe of the liver does suggest that, with other market indicators taken into account, returns should be good within a decade."

Pros
You and your family get to eat the sacrifice afterwards.

Cons
Messy, expensive, almost certainly unreliable.

Reading the stars

An astrologer examines the position of the stars and makes predictions based on whether or not Aries is rising in Capricorn, and what time of night the Moon comes up etc, etc...

What she said to Bibulous:
"You're a Virgo aren't you?" (He isn't.) "I can tell by your stern and scrubbed appearance. Hey, loosen up, man, you need to do some tantric yoga.

Your chart shows that Mercury rising in the house of Aquarius suggests that investing in the Armenian slave trade would be really far out."

Pros
Accepted three beads and a daisy as payment.

Cons
We wouldn't touch this with a barge pole. <u>AND</u> this stuff is **really** popular. We can't believe everyone takes it so seriously.

NEXT WEEK: HOW THROWING DICE CAN REALLY DECIDE YOUR FUTURE!

EMPIRE ESTATES

34 AQUEDUCT AVENUE, ROME

Luxury Town House

When only the best will do. A most elegant and centrally situated town house in Rome's choicest district. What more visible sign of authority could any senator, banker, businessman or general require?

- Impressive atrium for meeting and greeting guests.
- Decorative courtyard pool.
- Semi-transparent stone windows.
- Manageable walled garden.
- Most unusual and status-enhancing second floor, for family bedrooms.

- Shop at front of house, to rent out.
- Running water toilet.
- East facing study, giving bright morning light, and plenty of ventilation to prevent mildew occurring in paper and papyrus.

Potential buyers should note: This property has no bathroom, but there are public baths a short walk away.

RURAL PROPERTIES

VILLA

Only once in a century does a property as magnificent as this come on the market. "Dunrulin" in Etruria is the former home of a murdered and disgraced emperor, and Empire Estates is expecting a quick and competitive sale.

- Part of large estate producing olive oil and wine.
- Own baths, wine making area and granary.
- Beautifully decorated mosaics and murals.

ALSO ON THE MARKET

LARGE FARM

Maximize your profits with this magnificent farm in Apulia. Comes complete with staff and 300 slaves. Specializes in figs and wheat.

SMALL FARM

Every Roman dreams of a place away from the squalor and bustle of the city. What better place to start than this comfy three-room farm in Umbria.

EVEN SMALLER FARM

A property that's within reach of even the most humble buyer. Would suit extremely capable carpenter

---

ALL PRICES ON APPLICATION

BIG OLIVE APARTMENTS

The Forum Rome

APPLY WITHOUT DELAY

There's no place like Rome, and what better place to live than in a Big Olive apartment block. Rome has 46,000 of these Insulae blocks, and we've just built another ten of them.

✷ **No kitchens!** Why cook when inns and bars are so cheap and convenient? (Besides, who wants to burn the block down? Imagine your shame!)

✷ **No private toilets!** But what better place to complain about the state of your bowels than the apartment's standard 12 seater, open-plan public toilet bench. Sympathy guaranteed!

✷ **No running water!** Get super-fit carrying buckets of water up five flights of stairs. A conveniently nearby fountain provides a constant supply.

✷ **No peace!** All apartments have shops or taverns on the ground floor.

THE CONSUL DELUXE
First floor, expansive, stone walls, luxurious, balcony (but watch out for refuse and sewage being thrown from upper floors.)

THE CENTURION
Second floor standard accommodation, wood-burning braziers, big windows.

THE TRADESMAN
Top floor, wooden living spaces, small easy-to-heat rooms.

WE'RE POTTY ABOUT THESE STANDS

KITCHEN NEWS

Those lucky few readers who are rich enough to have a kitchen will be interested in these new utensils.

Increase the life of your cooking pots with these pottery and iron stands. Place directly between your hot charcoal stove and the pot of your choice, and hey presto, all the heat, with none of the wear and tear.

Strain those sauces with the all-metal Stranulus Strainer. Sturdy construction means it will survive the attentions of even the clumsiest slave.

Pot stands. So simple! So convenient!

WEDDING LATEST

• Most girls are waiting until they're 14 to get married now, although a few still take the plunge at 12 or even earlier. Medical chiefs are not happy with the trend. Death in childbirth is still all too common, and most experts agree that the younger the mother, the better chance of survival for both her and baby.

• Be sure to arrange your marriage for a good day on the calendar. Most weddings still take place in the second half of June, which is the luckiest time of the year.

• Our wedding day rituals are spreading! Placing the ring on the third finger, left hand, wearing a white wedding tunic, and having the groom carry the bride over the threshold of their new home, are all catching on throughout the Empire.

RECIPE OF THE DAY

ANCHOVY DELIGHT WITHOUT THE ANCHOVIES

It's happened to us all. You want to do a nice tangy anchovy dish, but there's none to be found at the market.
Your guests are waiting,
and they're getting impatient!

What do you do? Here's what...

1. *Take a good size pan and gently heat a fish sauce with a dash of pepper, a butter and flour roux, and a little olive oil.*

2. *Add four fillets of grilled fish (any white fish will do) and stir.*

3. *Gently fold in raw eggs to bind the mixture together.*

4. *Now – the magic ingredient. Add a good quantity of small jellyfish. (Much easier to get hold of than anchovies, and half the price.)*

5. *Simmer until well cooked.*

6. *Serve with ground pepper. Not one of your guests will guess you've run out of anchovies!*

Today's recipe comes from Apicus's Cookbook, available in all good bookshops now

cut out and keep

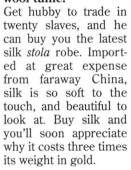

THE OPEN-ALL-HOURS
GOD SHOP

HELPING YOU DECIDE WHO'S WORTH A WORSHIP

A standard-issue Roman temple. Remember, a sacrifice in time saves nine!

YOU'RE SPOILED FOR CHOICE!!!

Religion in Ancient Rome has always been a pick-and-mix affair. We've got our own Roman gods and goddesses, and keeping them sweet is vital for the survival of Rome. Then we've got all sorts of other ones from the people we've conquered over the centuries.

We don't mind who else you worship, as long as you pay due respect to our state gods and the Emperor!

THE STATE RELIGION

Rite or wrong? Of all our gods and goddesses the state deities are the ones you've really got to watch out for. We've got temples dedicated to them all over Rome and if you don't say the occasional prayer, or offer the odd sacrifice, they won't protect you as you go about your daily business.

There are 14 or 15 really famous ones, and a whole bunch of lesser ones. (True, most of them have been adapted from the Greek models, but who cares? If the cap fits wear it!) Here's an overview of a few of the big cheeses to give you the general idea...

JUPITER

He's king of the gods, and the deity in charge of thunder and lightning. He's exactly like the Greek god Zeus, right down to his thunderbolt hurling, and his disgruntled wife, who's mad at him for carrying on with other goddesses behind her back, the rat!

NEPTUNE

God of the Sea, and identical to Poseidon in Greece. You pray to him if you are going on a voyage and don't want your ship to sink in a storm.

CERES

She's the goddess of agriculture, and the same as Demeter in Greece. You pray to her if you want your crops to flourish and your runner beans to sprout.

HOLIDAY TIME

As you know, each year there are over 100 public holidays and ceremonies here in Rome, devoted to venerating and celebrating these gods. They're a great opportunity to let your hair down, get staggeringly drunk, and stuff your face with top quality nosh. Our fave festivals here at the *Record* are:

•**Anna Perenna** on March 15, which celebrates the goddess of the year. On this festival some Romans believe you'll live for as many years as you can drink glasses of wine.

•**Saturnalia** on December 17, which is devoted to the God Saturn. We celebrate this by swapping places with our slaves for a day, and waiting on them at the dinner table.

HOUSEHOLD GODS

These are a lot more affable than the state gods. Each family has its own personal guardian spirit – called the *genius* – and each part of the house has its own little domestic god. For example there's **Janus**, who's the god of the doorway, and **Vesta**, the god of the hearth. You keep these gods happy by praying to them and leaving small gifts of wine, bread or fruit at the family shrine. (Make sure you do too – otherwise the door will start to jam, and the fire will be impossible to light!)

EXOTIC FOREIGN STUFF

Many Romans find the state gods a bit too distant, and not terribly reliable. After all, if you sacrifice an expensive sheep to Neptune to keep you safe at sea, and then your ship gets ravaged by pirates and you spend 30 years as a galley slave, it somewhat undermines Neptune's credibility. So, many Romans are turning to a variety of foreign gods and religions. Here are a few of them...

CYBELE

The ladies' choice. Cybele comes from Asia Minor and she's most concerned about fertility, healing and nature. Ceremonies to worship her include wild music and dancing, which sounds quite entertaining, and definitely more fun than leaving an over-ripe apple on the family shrine for the god of the doorway. (Is it any wonder he never takes it...?)

JESUS

Popular with poor people, Jesus promised his followers life after death. **This religion only believes in one god.** It's not a good one for anyone seeking a quiet life, as it's unpopular with the Roman government which requires citizens to worship the Emperor and state gods. Expect a lot of persecution.

MITHRAS

Top god with soldiers. Mithras comes from Persia and offers his followers life after death, which is quite a comfort when you're facing 20,000 fired-up barbarians all determined to hack your head off with a blunt axe. No women allowed in this religion.

ISIS

This one comes from Egypt. Isis became really popular in Rome when devotee Cleopatra came here in 45BC.

This religion involves paying homage to goddess Isis who rules heaven and earth and wheat and barley.

Lots of elaborate and mysterious ceremonies to keep you wondering what it's all about.

NUDITY AND VIOLENCE NOT ENOUGH
CLAIMS THEATRE OWNER

The theatre has long been popular in Rome. We may not be as highbrow as the Greeks – but who really needs brow-furrowing metaphysical tragedies about man's relationship with the gods when you can have comedies stuffed to bursting with gratuitous nudity and violence!

STIFF

But recently, theatres have been facing stiff competition from fatalities-guaranteed chariot racing and mega-death gladiator tournaments. But fear not, culture lovers – theatre managers know just how to win back the customers!

PEP PLAN

"I've been in this business for 25 years, and I tell you, you can't go wrong with nudity and fighting," said theatre manager Andrius Ludicrous Wetulus. "But the problem with nudity is that once you're there, you can't go any further. After all you can't be any more naked than totally naked.

"However, violence is **different**, and that's where we intend to **pep things up**. Check out our forthcoming attractions. We've got plays coming up with **real live crucifixions**, and **hands being chopped off**. Best of all, for one night only, we've got a production of *The Death of Hercules* where the actor playing Hercules is **burned alive at the end of the play!**

RED HOT

"Does he mind? I'm sure he does, but he's a convicted criminal and we've managed to persuade him that we'll do something FAR WORSE to him if he doesn't cooperate with this particular stunt!"

In Roman theatre, when the actors say "I'm dying out here", they really mean it!

NEXT WEEK: INTERVAL SNACKS – SPECIAL REPORT

THE RECORD SALUTES
THE GREEKS!!!

**The Greeks! What a classic bunch of fellows. As soon as we saw them we realized they deserved more than just conquest, exploitation and slavery.
So after we'd conquered them, exploited them and turned them into slaves, we COPIED their culture and ideas.
We're not daft, are we?
So join us in the *Record* guide to WHAT WE GOT FROM THE GREEKS!!!**

CITY LAYOUT

When we build a new city we build it on a grid system. That means all the streets are at right angles. This was invented by Greek town planner Hippodamus in 450BC. When we occupied Greek cities we liked the idea and adopted it immediately.

CITY STYLE

OK, we admit it. WE LOVE GREEK BUILDINGS. That sense of proportion, harmony and balance gets us every time! Our temples are almost carbon copies of Greek ones – probably because they're built by Greek craftsmen and architects. We swiped the Greek column style wholesale, but we've added a few home-grown Roman touches of our own.

INTERIOR DECORATION

Sigh. Those Greeks, they really know how to paint a room. We love a nicely decorated house, and no one does it better than a Greek interior designer. Mosaics, wall painting, figurines, the Greeker the better!

COINS

Ker-ching! Yes, when we saw they used money we copied that too. The first Roman mint opened in 269BC. (Different face on the coins, of course – we do have some imagination.)

GODS

We've adopted Greek mythology lock, stock and barrel. We've given them different names, but apart from that our top gods are exactly the same as the Greeks, right down to the little details. For example, they have god of wine Dionysus, a portly fun guy who likes to get drunk and have a good time. Our god of wine is portly fun guy Bacchus, who likes to get drunk and have a good time.

MEDICINE

Say alpha!! Yup, practically all our medical knowledge comes from Greek physician Hippocrates. We've even adopted the transparently ridiculous Greek technique of sleeping in temples to try and cure ourselves.

ART

Ever since we first looted a Greek city we've been crazy about Greek art – those lovely engraved plates, that inlaid furniture, and especially those statues. We bet there won't be better statue makers until the Renaissance.

EDUCATION

Even though we're top nation, and anyone of any importance in the Empire has to speak Latin, all our brightest boys have to learn Greek at school. This is because all the best books are written in Greek, and Greek literature and philosophy is a MAJOR influence on our own culture.

The best universities are in Athens and Rhodes in Greece, and the richest Romans still send their kids there to finish their education.

AND THAT'S NOT NEARLY THE END OF IT. WE HAVEN'T EVEN MENTIONED PUBLIC SPEAKING, PHILOSOPHY, ATHLETIC GAMES, COMEDIES, MUSICALS AND POETRY. HOW DO THEY DO IT???

EXCLUSIVE RECORD SERVICE

What could be more everyday than a slave? They're as commonplace as togas and aqueducts. But unlike togas and aqueducts, slaves have minds of their own. How do you stop them from running away? What stops THEM from killing YOU? How should they be punished when they DO misbehave? Top slave dealer Senula Severus answers your queries...

SENULA'S SLAVE SPOT

STUPID

Dear Senula,
I know it's a stupid question, but where do slaves actually come from? They've always been around, but they must have come from SOMEWHERE in the first place.

Mr Honorius Constantius, Ravenna

I always say slaves are people that fate has given a second chance. Many are barbarian warriors. Our soldiers could have killed them, but no, out of kindness they turned them into slaves. Then there are the provincials who've rebelled against Rome. They could have been executed for their impertinence, but no – they're slaves too.

Then there are people sentenced to death by the courts, and children who were left to die in the street because their parents couldn't feed them... they were picked up by kindly slave dealers and given a new chance in life. Oh, and all the children of slaves are slaves too.

SUBSTANCE

Dear Senula,
I am a gentleman farmer from Britannia. We don't have many slaves out there. I'm passing through Rome and I'd like to know how I go about buying one.

Mr Iacus Bullus, Rome

Owning just one slave is rather vulgar. Anyone of any wealth and substance has at least eight. Many landowners have over 500.

You can buy slaves privately or from slave dealers. An established dealer is probably your best bet, unless you know the private individual you're buying from.

A dealer will guarantee that your investment is not a runaway, has no criminal record, and is in good health. Buying older slaves is cheaper, but I always say buy young, so you get more out of them.

Pick one that looks as well as can be expected. After all, you don't want to waste money on faulty goods.

Once you've bought, you'll be given a certificate of ownership. This can also prove that your slave is not a runaway.

Alternately you might like to consider renting. Rental slaves, though, are usually in much worse condition, and likely to offer a poorer service.

SURLY

Dear Senula,
These slaves are a surly bunch. I'm always having to hit them to get them to set the curls in my hair correctly. Why just the other day I had to have my cook whipped because he'd overdone the rabbit we were having for lunch. The look he gave me! What I'd like to know is, what stops these crabby beggars from killing us in our beds?

Mrs Callus Catillus, Verona

The main thing that keeps a slave in his place is FEAR, and there are a whole range of punishments available to the slave owner to make sure his property doesn't get out of hand. If your slave runs away you can have him whipped or thrown to the lions. A slave who murders his master is put to death. All the other slaves in that household are executed too. This encourages slaves to report any murder plots they hear about to their master.

BUY OUT

Dear Senula,
I'm a slave and I've heard that it's possible for me to BUY my freedom. Tell me more!

Name and address withheld, Rome

Yes it's true. It's not just whips and crucifixion that keeps a slave in his place. Many farsighted owners offer the prospect of freedom to slaves who serve their masters particularly well. It's quite an encouragement to be good. Some owners even free their slaves out of the goodness of their hearts. Others let their slaves BUY their freedom, from any tips and gifts they may have scraped together over the decades.

What happens is that you and your owner make a declaration in front of a magistrate, and then you're free.

LETTER OF THE WEEK

SEDITIOUS

Dear Senula,
I'm puzzled by this slavery business. My friend Stocksus Shario, who knows a fair bit about economics, says that keeping slaves is just as expensive as hiring workers to do the sort of jobs that most slaves do.

So why do people go to the expense of buying slaves which they then have to house, feed and clothe?

Mr L. Logicus, Venicia

In truth, I'm not often asked this question. What a seditious person your friend must be! People like to own slaves because it gives them a sense of power. What could be more deliciously powerful than having complete life-or-death control over another human being who's completely at the mercy of your whim and fancy? Having slaves also increases your status in the community. It's nice to look down on someone else too. It makes you feel better about yourself.

NEXT WEEK. SLAVES AND ALCOHOL - WHAT EVERY OWNER SHOULD KNOW

ROLL UP! ROLL UP!
FOR 123 DAYS OF
BLOOD, GUTS, AND CRUELTY
EEEEUUUGHHH, IT'S DISGUSTING!!!

Chomp! Slurp! Munch! The beast show gets bestial. And this isn't the worst of it.

Says the *Record*'s sports correspondent Soccerus Bungus.

Gladiators – they've been part of Roman culture since the days of the Republic. At first they only fought at funerals, as people believed the dead needed some bloodshed to see them on their way.

Then politicians started featuring gladiator fights as part of the public entertainment they laid on when they wanted to show off how wealthy they were. Now we've even got a special venue for gladiator matches – the Colosseum – with seating for 50,000.

Most Romans JUST LOVE these games, so I'm really flying in the face of fashion when I say <u>it's all gone too far.</u>

I've just been to day 11 of Emperor Trajan's 123-day Games, currently being held to celebrate our victory over the Dacians. Here I witnessed an unparalleled display of the most appalling savagery this side of a half-starved, rabid werewolf feeding frenzy.

JUGGLE

At 10:00am there was an **Opening Procession**. Everyone watched a host of gladiators, dancers, jugglers, priests and musicians as they trooped past the Emperor.

The horror really began at 11:00am with the **Beast shows.** The rarest, most powerful and beautiful species on Earth were brought into the arena and set against each other, or a ragged selection of unfortunate humans.

What was even more repulsive was the audience.

They were **thrilled** at the sight of starving bears as they battled to the death with terrified elephants. They **gasped** with excitement as bewildered panthers and bulls mauled each other. Then they **cheered** as Christians, criminals and assorted prisoners of war, were thrown to starving lions and **EATEN ALIVE.**

I was feeling quite queasy after that, so I was relieved to see in the schedule that the next section of the show was **comedy and light entertainment**.

I was expecting clowns, and musicians, but what I got was two blind, chained together gladiators fighting each other to the death. The audience roared with laughter as they swiped the air with their razor sharp swords. The clowns came after, but by then I wasn't in the mood for a laugh.

UNHINGED

At 2:00pm it was the **Gladiators.** This was where the audience got the chance to yell like unhinged lunatics. Each day 20 pairs of assorted gladiators fight in one-on-one contests. They're recruited from prisoners, slaves, and do-anything-for-money freemen.

During a bout, each pair of gladiators fought each other to a standstill, and the winner stood over the loser with his sword pointing into his vitals. The crowd and the Emperor then decided his fate... If the loser fought well, they cheered and he was dragged off to fight another day. If he'd not put his heart into it, they brayed and howled and he was killed on the spot.

And that wasn't the end of it. At 5:00pm there was a **Sea battle.** During a short intermission, the arena was flooded, and two fleets of a thousand men (picked from the meanest criminals and prisoners of war they could lay their hands on) engaged in a REALISTIC SEA BATTLE, with real swords, arrows and spears. Needless to say, most of them ended up getting killed.

STEAM

I know us Romans like to let off a little steam – especially the poor and unemployed ones with a lot of time on their hands. But isn't it time we stopped all this? I left that evening feeling like I'd spent the day in the company of the most repulsive, odious creatures on earth – and I work for a tabloid newspaper!!!

FLYING KICK SPARKS

RACING RIOT

GAIUS IN DEEP TROUBLE AGAIN

Gaius (on horse with red plumes on head) takes a corner three laps into his 39th win.

Rioting chariot racing fans tried to beat three shades of stuffing out of each other at Rome's 250,000 capacity Circus Maximus yesterday.

Stadium authorities were forced to call in security staff to restore order.

ABUSE

The trouble started around 3:00pm when fans of the Blue team* started to hurl abuse at the Red team's controversial star driver – hothead Gaius Brutulus Aquitanius – who had just won his 39th race, and was leaving the stadium in triumph.

As he passed by, Blue fan Scabius Scragulus Scrumulus shouted out "Gaius Brutulus Aquitanius is a girly wimp who gives his horses lumps of sugar and puts pink ribbons on their tails."

SAVAGE

This was clearly too much for Gaius, a slave from Gaul, who leaped into the grandstand and replied with a savage flying head-kick. The incident ignited sections of the crowd, and a close quarters, hand-to-hand brawl erupted in various parts of the stadium. Racing was held up for half an hour while security staff attacked rioters with heavy wooden sticks, and cutting personal remarks.

ANGRY

Interviewed after the incident, Gaius's manager Ronus Ronulus admitted he was angry with his rider. "I didn't spend 30,000 sesterces buying him from the Greens in order to have him risk an injury attacking some cretin in the crowd. This sport is quite dangerous enough already. If he does it again he'll be whipped. Chariot racing is the nation's number one spectator sport, and this sort of conduct sets a very bad example. If fans want to see competitors behaving like bar-room brawlers they can go to a gladiator arena."

MOOD

But Gaius was in no mood to apologize. "Pah," he shrugged "what can they do. No one can balance on a flimsy wicker chariot quite like me, or take a corner so tightly without falling off, or control four wild horses with such finesse. My fans are the most loyal in the world, and if Ronulus has me whipped he'll have all the windows in his town house broken in the middle of the night...."

*Note to foreign readers. Our racing teams are divided into four stables of drivers, trainers, and horses. They are called the Reds, Greens, Blues and Whites.

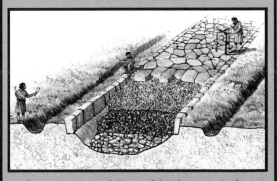
NEXT WEEK: THE SHOCKING TRUTH ABOUT BRIBES, TRAINERS, RIDERS AND HORSES...

WARM AS TOAST

THAT'S WHAT THEY'LL SAY WHEN YOU BUY A HOUSE WITH

HORATIUS CENTRAL HEATING

ECONOMICAL – Heat retaining pillars keep your house hot, even after the fires have gone out.

EASY – Just a few fires do all the work! Get your slave to keep them going.

SAFE – Say goodbye to the fire risk of an open grate and wooden floorboards.

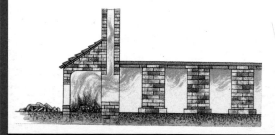

Especially recommended for citizens in Britannia and Northern Gaul, where the sun doesn't shine quite like it does in good old Rome.

ANNOUNCEMENTS

Attention, citizens of Rome. A major misunderstanding has occurred. We believe it was Remus that murdered Romulus, and then went on to found the capital city – **not the other way around**. Rome should be renamed Reme at once! Send your missives of support to: Spotterus Crankius, President, The Remus Society, 24 Basilica Avenue, Reme. TOGETHER, WE CAN CHANGE THE WORLD. Box 29

JOBS

WE NEED MEN
Due to a high turnover of staff, the Roman Fire Brigade seeks NEW RECRUITS. Some skill with bucket of water and sponge would be useful, but not essential. With our hot climate, rickety wooden apartments and open fires, YOU'LL NEVER BE BORED!!! Box 31

FOR SALE

OLD GOAT
Hours of fun with the pet you can milk and fleece. Guaranteed never to bite or butt. Box 36

HAIR
Beautiful blond tresses – ideal for a wig. From recent consignment of freshly delivered Goths. (No more fun for them.) Box 39

"SLAVES! SLAVES! SLAVES!"
The one-stop shop, for all your slavery needs. Box 41

PICTURE CREDITS

Ancient Art and Architecture Collection, Ltd (14, 15); **Barnaby's Picture Library** (30); **C.M.Dixon** (8, 18); **e.t. archive** (17 – Pantheon, Paris); **Werner Forman Archive** (12 – Museo Nazionale Romano, Rome); **Scala Photographic Agency, Florence** (Front cover).

Every effort has been made to trace the copyright holders of material in this book. If any rights have been omitted, the publishers offer to rectify this in any subsequent editions following notification.